John Thompson's
Easiest Piano Course

PART SEVEN

The Willis Music Company

Foreword

PART SEVEN develops gradually in all directions — musically and pianistically. The various staccato and legato Touches find ample opportunity for application as well as the attack and release of long and short slurs.

There are many examples in Rhythmic Form as represented by Marches and various Dance Rhythms, including several Syncopated Rhythms.

Examples in Lyric Form include the Nocturnes, Folk Tunes and Airs from the Operas, etc.

TECHNIC

When pupils have advanced this far, they show a wide variance in Technical needs. Therefore, it is quite impossible to place Etudes in just the exact spot in the book to meet the requirements of all pupils.

To meet this problem, there are six Etudes at the end of the book, beginning on page 41, which are intended to be assigned as the pupil progresses through PART SEVEN, wherever, in the teacher's opinion, they will do the most good.

If additional technical work is indicated, a supplementary book should of course be assigned. In this connection, it is suggested that the author's TUNEFUL TECHNIC, Books 1 and 2, will fit the material in this book perfectly.

SOLO PIECES

For a list of solo pieces and additional supplementary teaching books particularly suited for pupils in this grade level, the teacher is urged to refer to a COMPLETE REFERENCE CATALOG OF ALL JOHN THOMPSON EDITIONS in the Willis Catalog.

This may be obtained without cost by writing to The Willis Music Company — 7380 Industrial Road - Florence Kentucky 41022-0548

The COMPLETE REFERENCE CATALOG OF ALL JOHN THOMPSON EDITIONS is an excellent guide for materials commensurate with the pupil's progress.

John Thompson

Contents

W. M. Co. 7396

The correct metre for this piece is really 9/8. But for convenience in reading, it has been scored in 3/4.

After it is learned, try to increase the tempo until you can play it with *one count to the measure* when the metronome is set at 96.

The piece is descriptive in style. Be sure to observe all accent and staccato marks, etc.

The Burro

Allegro vivace ($\mathbf{.}$ = 96)

6

W.M.Co. 7396

Play this piece in a whimsical, carefree manner. Toss off all the phrases sharply, and make as much contrast as possible between staccato and legato.

The repeat mark at the end of the piece, *Dal Segno al Fine,* means return to the sign (%) and play to *Fine.*

Street Carnival

This old Italian Folk Song is popular the world over.

Play as expressively as possible, and give the melody your best singing tone.

Follow all pedal and phrasing marks carefully, and play the broken chords in the accompaniment with a rolling motion of the hand and forearm.

Santa Lucia

Italian Folk Song

The most important factors in a March are Rhythm and Tempo. Sharp accents will establish a well-defined rhythm, and steady, even counting will insure the regular flow of the Tempo.

Be sure to give enough importance to the left-hand notes having double stems — one up and one down. They suggest the Trombones of the band and have almost the significance of a secondary theme.

Victory March

As with all your pieces marked *alla breve,* learn this one first counting four to each measure. Later as speed develops, begin counting two to each measure (one count to each half note).

Since this number is in dance form, rhythm is of course uppermost. Be sure, therefore, to observe everything that will help point up the rhythm such as accents, slurs, staccato, etc.

Tango

The Mazurka is a Polish dance which dates back to the 16th Century.

It differs from the Waltz in that the accent usually occurs on the third beat — or sometimes on the second beat as in the following piece.

Be sure to observe all accents and slurs as they form a most important part of the interpretation.

Mazurka

A powerful syncopation results when the accents are applied strictly as marked in the following piece. They are easy to play, however, when it is remembered that in the first two measures of each line (first page) the accents always fall on the same key (D), and are played by the thumb each time.

Syncopatin' Sam

D. C. al Fine

W.M.Co. 7396

This piece is a novelty in that it is built almost exclusively on the Chromatic Scale. In the first theme, an ascending chromatic figure is repeated over and over while the second theme, page 21, is in the left hand and consists entirely of notes of the Chromatic Scale descending.

Valse Chromatique

Rhythm is uppermost in this piece.

Pay strict attention to all accents, slur signs, staccatos, etc.

Learn it first in four-four, then gradually increase the tempo until you can play it at the speed indicated, counting two to the measure.

Flight to the Moon

Ignace Leybach was a pianist, born in Gambshiem, Alsace.

He studied under several masters, including some piano instruction under Chopin in Paris.

He composed light, drawing-room pieces which became very popular. The following example is probably the most popular of all his pieces, and still occupies a prominent place in the list of salon music.

Nocturne means "Night Song," which gives a clue to the interpretation. Note that the middle section becomes more animated after which a return is made to the first theme, and the piece ends on a Coda played a little more slowly and very softly.

from

Fifth Nocturne

I. Leybach
(arr.)

W.M.Co. 7396

The Polonaise is more ot a procession than a dance. It was used in Poland as the nobles marched in stately fashion before the throne.

The original metre of a Polonaise is 3/4 but, for convenience in reading, this example has been scored in 2/4 — *each measure representing one beat of the original.* Follow all accents and slur signs faithfully as they are essentially part of the rhythm.

from
Polonaise, Op. 53

Frederic Chopin
(arr.)

Here is a little "Rhapsody in Black" in which the right hand plays on black keys only.

The piece is written on the Pentatonic Scale. The Pentatonic Scale is a five-note scale having no 4th or 7th. It is sometimes called the Scotch Scale because most Scotch folk tunes are based on it. However, it was also used by the Chinese.

When the following example has been learned, it will be good practice to transpose it to G major, one half-step higher.

PRELIMINARY EXERCISE

Black Key Study

With Colors Flying

In the following example, the melody passes from one hand to the other. However, it should be easy to follow as it is shown in large notes. Properly played, it should sound like a cello solo.

Simple Aveu

Francis Thomé
(arr.)

Tempo I

p dolce

poco rall.

pp a tempo

pp

ppp

The Soft Shoe Dancer

W.M.Co. 7396

For convenience in reading, the first line is scored on four staves.

Hymn to the Sun

from the Opera, "The Golden Cockerel"

Rimsky-Korsakoff
(arr.)

The six Etudes following are intended to be assigned, at the discretion of the teacher, as the student progresses through this book.

Etude, No. 1

42

Etude, No. 2

Etude, No. 3

Etude, No. 4

W.M.Co. 7396

Etude, No. 5

Etude, No. 6

Certificate of Merit

This certifies that

....

has successfully completed

PART SEVEN
OF
John Thompson's
EASIEST PIANO COURSE
and is eligible for promotion to

PART EIGHT

....

Teacher

Date ....